Days Beside Water

for Jenny

Days Beside Water

Gregory O'Brien

CARCANET

First published in Great Britain in 1994 by
Carcanet Press Limited
208-212 Corn Exchange Buildings
Manchester M4 3BQ

A CIP catalogue record for this book is available
from the British Library.
ISBN 1 85754 047 6

The publisher acknowledges financial assistance
from the Arts Council of Great Britain

Typeset and printed by University Printing Services,
Auckland, New Zealand

Contents

The New Zealander

Considered the fastest vessel sailing out of Sydney at the time (1836), the brigantine The New Zealander, *of 200 tons register, derived her name from her figurehead, which was a striking carved figure of a New Zealander, the name by which the Maoris were then known. Having loaded a cargo of maize and pork for the return voyage to Sydney, the boat lay at anchor at Table Cape, Mahia Peninsula, when a heavy sea and strong wind set in. After the anchor cable had chafed in two on the rocky bottom, the brigantine tacked about for some time, but, as she did not make any headway, another anchor was dropped. The wind subsided, but the heavy sea caused the chain cable to part, and the vessel was driven on the rocks, to become a total wreck. The crew landed the following morning and experienced the additional misfortune of having everything, including their clothing, taken from them.*

CARCANET

PRESS LTD 208-212 Corn Exchange Manchester M4 3BQ   phone 061 834 8730   fax 061 832 0084

REVIEW COPY *We have pleasure in enclosing this book for review*

DAYS BESIDE WATER by Gregory O'Brien
To be published on: 20th January 1994
£7.95 net   80 pages   230 x 160 mm   ISBN 1 85754 047 6

If you require any further information please contact Janet Allan at Carcanet

1 Falls

Albert Pinkham Ryder

(Moonlight Marine)

In the uncontrollable
    late afternoon
        stillness I struggle

with Marion for control
    of the dinghy.
        As the world wanders

muttering across its
    sky. Her good heart
        in spite of battles

remembers only Spring —
    'the twilight orchestra'
        asleep at the piano —

other days, thousands of
    flowers would colour
        the dunes orange and green

down to high water
    mark where the grey
        ocean burst

with the orange
    and the green
        of jellyfish.

*

Shadows cross the water
    and we are wholly
        covered, moonlit,

marine, out of breath
　　of vapour trails
　　　　this dinghy eluding

both of us. Later to run aground
　　amidst the pale
　　　　architecture, a

sprinkling of hills, where
　　the sloping field becomes
　　　　a wall, a door

or window opening
　　on the soft lawn
　　　　of Marion

　　and Marion.

A recipe for custard

These are the things
that keep us together:
the blue mountains

a musician dozing
against the elephant
tree, clarinet

embedded in blue soil.
Morning reaches this
far, touches evening

the Hydro Majestic
a palace overthrown
by leaves. Nights

made of canvas, stretched
to any length and held
there, bath-water golden

from the clay reservoir.
We dream an orchestra
asleep outside

on the tennis courts
hear the concrete dolphin
swim across an ancient

pool, and wonder if the
cable-car will reach
the Three Sisters,

how far these mountains reach
down into the ground.
By morning the orchestra

will be out of work,
the ballroom will resume
its emptiness

another year. And
the musicians will hide
the concrete dolphin in

the back of a van which
by late afternoon
will have reached

the coast. We will
follow in the evening
find them on a beach

gathering kelp
they will take home
and share as custard.

Blue Mountains, NSW

The Ten Most Beautiful Women In The World

Flying junk, clouds thrown from the tops
of buildings, where we find ourselves

lost between uncomfortable bars, the moon clearing
a patch beneath our skin, a longing

or long arcade where we search our pockets
to find a coin small enough for a rusted slot-

machine, a converted pinball or one
armed bandit. We have not seen our mother

in eleven months, but have lately found
The Ten Most Beautiful Women In The World

in 3D. A shutter twitches, and night outside
becomes night inside their hotel or

emporium. A coin drops into the upholstered
darkness. The machine's two eyes

staring into our two eyes. Then, faded
into her background, (1) a woman

in a vast bikini, c.1950, only the pink material
remaining, brighter than ever,

hovering, almost, in space. (2) following: a lime-
green outfit, the colour touched

by hand. A fizzing bulb has faded (4), (5) and (7)
completely. (6) has melted down. Only the

artificial colours remain, these costumes like
flags of modesty. (10) dissolves into milk,

then a shutter snaps. And it is night again
inside The Ten Most Beautiful Women In The World.

Marsden at Matapouri

1

An arranger of shrubs, a wind
to weigh anchor on . . .

*As mine is to dream, and make
my own*, said Marsden
at a child's desk
        a lover of coasts,
conversions. Who would make a kite
from the paper-thin bark
        of a tropical tree.

*As a seagull to acquire grace
a sparrow to perseverance
    a hawk to deliverance
a crane to eloquence,*
        who keeps

her earrings around the perimeter
of the hand-basin
        a wedding gift once
the waves' overlapping —
        while

one morning on deck she
    trimmed his beard
over the water. Who was counting
waves, remembering window-boxes.
        Out to pasture

the last good while, she said,
their passion an allowance,
        shipboard —
who watches a twisted palm
    on the foreshore
and what might grow there, *the two
of us on a great bough*, as seeds
blowing across a field

in search of the trees
    they were to become.

You have talk in you, she
would say
      Maestro Kettle!
and keep him
in mind
      Monsieur!
having a mind
to that

  . . . and how
when the long boat returns
    for them . . . .

2

Her shoulder, her secret.
Who combed his hair,
    trimmed his beard,
   pulled his teeth,
would wait for him in church,
the stained glass beyond.

Tend your valley, he would
    tend his flock,
      linger on a hillside,
a ribbon of sand —
souls divided on a map

as any good missioner —
    their fortunes made
of this. He would attend his office
and then
      her neck
a while, their cool bodies
trickling together at Matapouri Bay.
How do you tell a black-fronted
    from a caspian tern?
she asked. *You look at it!*

Later they would fall together
        and exclaim *My*

pumpkin boy!   My little shoe!

And every time this happened
it was as if a child
        in a distant country
was made a king.

3

Unlike Parkinson, he would say —
        himself a more occasional surveyor
of coastlines, the tide
        and outlying rocks —
his eyesight was never much
        except well-read, bespectacled.
He would watch as she swam,
shouldering the waves, facing shore

as if to always look
at him, but
        to conceal, in fact,
a tattoo on her shoulder blade
her husband never once saw.

Together only at night and usually
begowned against winter,
        or she would
wedge herself between branches
        to conceal it,
or bury her shoulder
in the sand, and Marsden's eyes
        unaccustomed to the sunlight . . .
There were friends, women
she would show the tattoo:

*A palm, to beg
your acquaintance, a tree*

and they, themselves
exiles from persimmons, among other things
      cast up,
some would say ruined
   on a southern shore.
They would gather beneath its leaves.

4

Skin bruised by
sunsets, kowhai

and the tide one finger
touching her lip, she would
attend her palm
    in secret
while he ministered to
the fainthearted, the hopeful,
   their failing farms,
     trading stations,
gloryboxes full of navigational
equipment. Flat-footed hills
walked beside them, streams
he named for her
   and after her, his memory palace
where he lived in
hope
   and the realisation
of hope.

To find admirers! she said —
persimmon seedlings following
them on these walks, and

trees at day's end,
his failing sight. Later he took
   to charting, in his retirement,
areas of coastline,
places they were together.

   Lord above!

Down below!

Unlike Parkinson, he would say
   hulls would never split
on his miscalculations; changes in tide,
current, geology would never be blamed
     on him. *Unlike Parkinson!*
He would not be dead of malaria,
out of Batavia
     and buried at sea
facing England. His lord a scent,

a particular rose. And all that time,
the voyage out,
   trips all over the country,
never to know
     or need to know
her secret, a shoulder blade
     a palm.

Matapouri Bay, Northland

18

Stray

1

A day knowing no
    impediment

or lovesome broadcast
    a distance
        you could cover

with one hand
    a cat descending

your clothes
    gathering them between
        claws, taking them to

a finer place.

2

    The curtains intervene

again, someone arranging
    their kisses like
        objects on a glass table

for you to hold so close
    or stray from.

Portrait of a painter and 'The world in front of the dog'

Blue alphabet
washed up beneath
Red Rocks, this

electricity inspector
sketched in autumn,
his name hidden

among fishing nets,
his folding chair
with paintbox

setting time
in fine voice
to it.

Labouring details,
the work-van as blue
as 'longing

for forgetfulness',
April, a truck spilling
burning newspapers

along the esplanade,
seals dozing in kelp,
the seasons

moving around him
as four impervious gulls
reaching for this

'pleasing arrangement
of forms', these days
decorated

with pencils,
eyelashes, 'failed
love', a long lunch

midriver before
vanishing off the face
of things.

Owhiro Bay, Wellington

Falls

Ending with storms
in the perfect costume
of an autumn

the sun made fast
by riderless waves —
a wedding among

sand dunes on a windy day
the dunes unfolding, moving
around the guests.

To while these afternoons
away alone, the boy
to follow

in your footprints
a while, or run ahead.
An American on the beach

won't walk with us
to the waterfall
('in the States we make

waterfalls, but can't
manage oceans').
This afternoon

a small country, how could
I miss you there?
To think of the weather

as always this fine
which might explain the
long lives of flowers

on the table, a vine
growing over the
Volkswagen, two roadside

signs, one announcing
JESUS WILL RETURN
the words added:

'to surf Raglan'
and another:
JESUS SAVES

'stamps'. To move
these half-truths to
truth, this man outside

shovelling in the ground
car parked among music-stands
a boy carrying a wooden

coffin containing
a trumpet. Between you
and me, everything

we know, a small country
of charms, virtues, how could
I miss you there?

for Marsden Hartley

Old Man South Road, 11 — 14

11 Wayne Brown's Endless Summer

To get out on the water, according
to Wayne, *not a beach break, a left*

hander off the Head . . . 'Black's was too big,
Last Chance a good swell, four and a half metres

after a cyclone near Fiji last month, kept
sucking all the water out of the bay,

left you staring straight down past the tip
of your board at the reef. Almost enough to make you

stay on the beach. Like Wayne's baby boy who fell
off a rock last season, swam around upside down

underwater, swallowed a few mouths full. Wayne
had to wrestle him back off a wave. The boy's

still terrified, can't even get him into the bathtub
now . . . A good thing, though, to be scared of water.'

*

To get back on these waves at Last Chance
last year. 'Two seconds to make up your mind

about a wave — get on it or off it. Wayne took a
drop, crushed a vertebra, had to be carried

out, concussed. A few weeks later I saw him
on the Lyall Bay bus, taking three rows of seats.

He had bought a new board.
Launched it.'

12 The cousin on the gravel verge

While not a thinker,
he says, he has
his thoughts, can jump

his mother's house on
a motorcycle.
Aged sixteen, has 'goosed'

six cars, owned one once,
'totalled it'
on a gravel road driving

back from the car yard —
'a good car,
you should have seen how,

a fifty metre drop, it
took it' —
limped five miles

home, 'didn't have
a licence,
couldn't wait for the police'.

*

'A week later the three
of us
doing 120 down

Five Mile Hill, dropped
her on loose
metal . . . In bed

five days with shock. But
only one broken
arm — the girl's — between

the three of us. And
the bike, goosed
that one as well.'

13 Maureen among ice men

They come to stay in her
motel — air men, ice men, mainly
engineers awaiting polar flights,

often delayed by conditions, cloud
cover. Americans who, laughing, say
they are tired of seeing Maureen's husband

'slugging from a bottle' ('something Dave
wouldn't even dream of doing!'), give her
a decanter and six glasses with

A N T A R C T I C A frosted around
them, a suggestion of icescape
come to rest, now, among Maureen's dried

arrangements. 'They're good boys, they're
softies, these eighteen stone men. If
they want to fight they go two blocks away.

Sure, they drink, they disappear
for days . . . The weather clears, they fly off.'
They get along well with the Japanese

professors who share their motel. One
English professor from Tokyo, who stayed
last August, still writes Maureen

the most exquisite letters, his English
'so beautiful and well written',
she says, 'it's just like *prose*'.

26

14 I have a neighbour who keeps moving the boundary posts

Seen them wash
   across the lawn
her entries into
   my green diary

exclamation marks
   pin-stepping, in formation
from east to
   my western house

my lake recedes
   soon I'll lose the stream
where my clay hut
   trickles

gone, my dock
   my buoys
my seepage, my
   run-off

when I leave there'll
   be no place left
one boundary touching
   the other

I'll go native
   bush, still
pursued,
   polished white

sure as
   her troubles,
her lavender
   neighbour mine.

The orchardists

What might be, among friends
an orchard, this horizon
    of vines, where sunlight tilts

the house and boys roll out
onto the lawn, a girl.
    If the ocean found them

here, the world a steep place
they might fall from (as life
    is for the slipping away)

a note left on the table:
All gone to beach.
    Are you with us?

    for Nicholas Jones, Waihi

One Among Many

They all look eighteen,
indifferent, their cats playing
among driftwood,

their rust-coloured town.
As a garden cultivates
calm, certain

weather
paints and repaints
these walls,

stands
the sky up and
knocks it down.

If they don't look
eighteen, they probably are
eighteen, in their

damned old town.
If they awaken at four,
their yellow hair

is knotted
so they sleep
until seven

then enter
each corridor, flowing,
without complication.

What they add
to this house, their
windows among us,

cultivating these
plains, certain rooms
belonging to

swans. And you,
also, look eighteen,
out on your

western wing,
walking the quiet voices
of the verandah,

your hair like dust in
sunlight, reminding us of
the one thing.

'The Spirit of the Realm of Flowers'

Old river-beaten hulls,
the child-nun and her cripples.
They slept in a boatshed

a hundred years
outstretched, reminded
of breezes,

the bend where the road
rolled over in its sleep,
fell into the river,

long tables of breakfast
cherries. Our father says
the rapids — he is

possessed by them —
from Pipiriki to Jerusalem,
they are our ancestors

talking among themselves.
And Grace is a long high
room, let us

defend its fire-
places, mirrored floors.
Evening paddling

towards Jerusalem, water
bearing its lilies, its scars —
river enough

for us — where
the landscape shrugs
a gravel road

off its back.
We are blessed and
we are gone.

Interludes beside water

1 Naval

You stand
in the presence
of 'great men'

great trees, their
hives, and these that
children pass

in rivers, floods,
on long slides, with
a fragrance of

hyacinths competing
with an old paintbrush
in a turps jar.

Here we have a
six-year son, the pleasant
formations of helicopters,

a battleship at Queen's
firing blanks at
the Eastbourne ferry,

this anniversary regatta
of everything, the beach
that climbs into your hair.

And long may
these clouds remain
clouds. Tomorrow even

we will feel the pinch,
separating, with skill,
the day's dreaming

from the day,
the long slide,
what was said.

2 Pools

Over-ripe with
shadows, the jacaranda tree,
a table with fruitbowl

like the Braques
some love. Unpredictable
as the man with

fixed expression,
the parliament of
children

'in for the swim',
wanting to *impress*
like politicians

to be *grown up*.
Waist-deep, waist-high
you tell me

rivers are melted
mountains, over your head
facing the Rimutakas

where's snow, clouds
'government', a man in red
shorts turning

the red fire-hose on
all of you. Later
the creatures

are reunited beneath
a river, a house
runs after a woman —

in books reaching from
one side of the bedroom
to the other —

summer's end,
children hosed off
the steps,

their spines
have touched, you
give up

a little.

for Jack-Marcel, Wellington

34

The Milk Horse

*for Sr Rita Hickey, and in memory
of Rewi Crichton, whose thoughts these grew from*

I have just read your account, Sister,
of our dear Mother's life and there
and then I became, as most people would say,
reminiscent, in truth I am
once more transported
back to Jerusalem . . . .
Morning astride a horse, the hills white
in the mist and still far away.
It is Jerusalem again. Here, the willows,
the buckets of cream, children passed
between the tops of cherry trees,
the river then the track then the road,
the cutting through the hill. Once again
I am leading the milk horse home
and having to run to keep ahead
for darkness comes quickly here . . . .
Reading your account, Sister,
I find myself running
back to Hiruharama.

A home of compassion

Safe from floodwaters, the Home of Compassion rested on top
of a small hill overlooking the Whanganui River. The Maori
contingent settled on upper river flats which were occasionally
flooded. Sometimes the church would appear to have been set
afloat on the river-mist which obliterated the pa quite often
until late in the day, when the church would be set down again
on the hilltop. The village below was constantly teeming with
hundreds of warriors who lived communally and were subser-
vient to a young Maori prince.

The milk horse

Leading the aged pack-horse from the convent to the farm for milk and back, there were times we had to stop to allow a pack of wild pigs to pass. I was seven or eight years old and trying, desperately, to calm a frightened horse! My worst fear, however, on these excursions was the flapping of ghost-like wings coming from behind me — a clucking Great Bird which would peck at my legs. For such emergencies, I carried a stick to fend the 'peka' off. Sometimes, when bulls and cows got in our way, I would climb upon the load on the horse's back and, scared, I would make myself concentrate on the clanking of the milk-cans. And I would imagine every other living and non-living creature in the valley, likewise, concentrating on that sound. Walking the three miles back to Hiruharama was always easier, the horse no doubt smelling the nose bag awaiting him at home. Gradually we would be back among the cherry trees, the darkness following on our heels.

Devotions

Summer, we would sleep in sacks dangling from rafters in the store; and the potatoes which covered the floor, three feet deep, gave off a warmth we could feel ascending the darkness, mingling with our sleep. While outside we heard the wild cows, the croaking of toads and Fr Soulas, the French priest, saying the Latin prayers, the church crammed with Maoris who, despite their warlike appearances and tattooed decorations on face and bodies, attended Evening Devotions and Sunday Mass.

A 'lapse'

Once, having said goodbye to her three hours earlier at the Home, Mother Aubert was at the farm when I arrived. Heralding my arrival with hungry cries, I tethered the horse and ran into the kitchen. On entering the room, however, I was scooped up off the clean earth floor and quietly ushered from the poor abode by one of the sisters expressing sad and gentle reproaches. Mother Aubert was in a trance. I remember seeing her that fleeting moment, lying on a couch, as if dead, with both eyes wide open. The Sisters were agitated and anxiously praying for her recovery. No doubt these trances, or 'lapses', were common in those days.

'Meri'

Wild demonstrations down at the pa were frequent. It was what Mother called 'the native enthusiasm'. Watching from the hilltop, we would imitate the frightening but picturesque festivities, the wild-pig killings, tangis, poi and rukuhuia dances. I would take letters from the good Mother down to the pa to the chief who was a Catholic. There were as many dogs as there were people at the pa — all manner of half-breeds which barked and snarled around me. But, on account of Mother Aubert's example, I would show no fear. Mother was a truly remarkable lady whose only love and affection, beside that for her god, was for 'the poor Maori and my children the poor'. The Maoris called her 'Meri', chanting vigorously, often according to the tempo of their paddles. Mother would succour the Maoris, visiting villages and fern huts by horseback. I went with her by foot or horse to many wild and inaccessible places, amidst friendly and unfriendly natives. Her life was threatened, I am sure of this now, but she knew no fear.

An offertory

We boys would accompany the Maoris when they set off in
canoes to catch wild geese and other poultry. They sang and
chanted songs and war cries as they paddled the long canoes,
later to glide swiftly home to prepare feasts which we would
attend with the Mother and Sisters all sitting cross-legged
around a central mat loaded with food. Chiefly the Maoris ate
pork, sweet potatoes and fish, often whitebait which abounded
in the river. Mother would frequently dispatch parcels of fruit
to the pa from the convent orchard.

'Au revoir' on the Whanganui River

When time came to say 'au revoir', we would all go down to the
paddle boat, hundreds of Maoris assembling along the river
banks and many more in canoes. The air thick with birdsong
and 'au revoir' from hundreds of tattooed faces.

A solemnity

I might have been eight or nine when Mother Aubert took me
and another boy with her to the Home of Compassion, Buckle
St, Wellington, where there were other children, not all of them
disabled, but most of them orphans. The Island Bay Hospital
was in construction and I remember standing alongside Mother
Aubert at the opening ceremony. I huddled close to her, terri-
fied by the large concourse of people, more white than brown.
I clung to her large gown wherever I went, even in the company
of her own Sisters or any of the clergy.

A restoration

I stayed at the Home in Buckle St adjoining a creche where
working mothers left their babies to be cared for by the Sisters
during the day. I became friendly with another boy who was
taller and older but had one side of his body bigger than the
other. Mother took great concern with his plight and I believe
it was her wonderful medicines and miraculous powers that
were responsible for his complete restoration. He, as I am told,
grew into a 'prince of a man' who, until his death, continued to
give valuable service, putting Mother Aubert's books in order.
He married happily, and his children were born to him in good
health.

A reprise

The canoes that followed us downstream when we left Jerusalem, I can see them as though they are still following me, gliding forth in the midst of farewells. And floating after us down the Whanganui River: 'au revoir', a trail of words leading back to Hiruharama.

If I can remember only details of those years,
Sister, it is because, as a child at Jerusalem,
I inhabited only details. The entire scene,
the view containing hills, the church, pa
and sweep of river were incomprehensible
to me. But how clearly I can recall Mother
going from bed to bed, down the aisle of boys —
she would kiss each one of us good night
on his bare chest and say
'I worship the Trinity in you'.
When adopted by Mother and her Sisters
I was, apparently, undernourished
and small for my age. My eyesight never
fully recovered. But, if I remain short-sighted
to this day, I still have no trouble
looking back! For, as darkness comes quickly here,
my memories are bathed in such light,
Sister, such light!

Rev. Brother John Rewi Crichton
Christian Brother, Adelaide, 12 May 1932

2 The rockstrewn hills

Wedding of the measel

Note: This poem has a source in Thomas Merton's 'Rites for the extrusion of a leper'. A measel is another name for a leper.

1

Out of what urgency
a deadness arisen
      on the surface of
this man, his affliction

his sickness like birds
      flying around the wings
of an aeroplane.

This man, his ceremony
a wedding ring on a stick
      or dead branch
he throws into the sandy distance
the guests he cuts
    out of a magazine
wind-blown aspects of a seaview
or romance, a beauty
    almost nautical. He navigates
a pool where everything
sparkles. Almost.

2

This man, his affliction
grass growing on
      a steep incline
or concavity. A charm

or uncertainty, the lean bough
of a wife

breaches the atmosphere
    his temperament

43

all that passes between
his skin
     and the desert.

3

Rendered incurable
this man, his obeisance
     gracious, recurrent
a desert by its barrenness.

The guests throw presents
down-wind to him
   dull blue streamers.
A wedding he chanced upon

and it was his. Lips
of stone, layers of pebbles
    across a dry creek bed.
His wife swims there. To be.

4

Is not to be missed —
a new layer of skin, the wind
   its speedy pardons

an uncommon deposit
a priest as hard as stone
   an aspect of the wind's
emptiness.

A woman take this
   plant in a handpainted pot
this desert grows
dead things. Overtaken by it

he dwindles, his ancestors visible now
identifiable in the soil, its momentary

moistness. Breached by their customs

44

there is only one way to grow
out here, inwards.

5

This man, his compliment
the distant voices
of near objects, their webs.
He is a volunteer of these zones
his sickness bigger than

his body, the constellations busy with it.
What the desert designates
as trees
the poem designates as wedding guests.
They scoop up the body's resistance, its weeping.

6

The measel, taken from his home
is given a house
easy access for the infirm
a dry branch
for a wife
you could cherish

or break. The nightsky
of electricity
distant transmission
of signals
you could take
for affection, the uneasy traffic
of a glance
across the surface of his skin.

7

A distance maintained
observed
there is something missing
inside him he identifies

as a crow
fluttering about the horizon.
A forecast. He will take her
dreamy effigy home
        to his dung mansion
tame animals will steal across
her shoulders as his eyes, their sinking
        accelerate down
the faint-hearted aisle.

8

Hardly a mild climate, with children
running out of the undergrowth
        sacred to the memory of

right now — holy rainwater
sprinkled on his forehead
        bowed, bowl upraised
his face a form of address.
The ceremony involves
living a while longer
    a woman take the duration of it

a spiked blanket. Oh love
oh desolate tree, how he is
        bound to it
isolate, he volunteers his vows
his skin is the surface of the world
    an acolyte, he is offered
incense and out of its burning
he fashions another self. An end to it.

9

Where is his wife his widow to be
she for whom his heart
        gongs
incandescently, for whom
its percussion
plays in the small moaning hours.

Where is she for whom
he swallows the dry fruit
        whole
for whom the twitch
of a bare
branch holds the closest embrace.

10

And died a fond man, rid of poets

was buried under his floor
    the house raised, well filled in.
But where is the bride, the widow
of these scars?

They cannot catch
the desert's ambassador
        she floats across the fiery
face of their need for her
the real estate
    of her affections
his infirmity, her bride.

It was night by then.

View from where we were sleeping

A hillside's rain. Beneath this
weather, we lie under mohair — dry,
glistening. The red mailman's coat

reflected wafting across the ceiling,
within sight of daffodils, a man in
a runabout dangling from a crane,

ten metres above the wharf, outboard whirring
in mid air. We could be strolling
under such strange machinations

of cloud, like the pale woman, his wife,
pushing a pram into the wind, her dream's
boat or barge high above her,

heading sunward past the Women's Aglow
handclapping meeting — well-trodden paths
flown over, patterns taken flight —

by wine or fresh loaves summoned.
Past Sister Brendan hidden behind a
cluster of flowers her height, also

leaning into the wind, herself soon
come to rest, gone too. Rain sinking
into its own history, the history

of those nearest us, resting
forehead to foreshore, beside these
misty waters, this rocking dredge.

Wellington

Tumbler

She wears a hat
seldom referred to
   as Mercy you might
have guessed the rim
pulled lower than her

eyes but watch her leap
the piano-stool, sparks fly
   from the clay pots
her bones whistle with these
rare and sought-after feats

you hear that crackle
the grand finale, her hands:
   she is taking
your house apart
in mid air.

Napoli, 32 Vedute

The hill down to Castel Dell'Ovo
walking home reading 'Adventures in Paradise'

in the half light when 'the edifying architecture'

becomes the eddying architecture.
What is this that keeps returning

these dull spectacular clouds

that moves my thoughts of you
from this breakwater

in slanting light, the fine sea?

To sleep to be nearer you, evenings
written on the backs of photographs

propaganda for loneliness, 'Sempre Amore'

'Azure', the hiss of trains
where sleep will come, a milk-truck full

of agile boys. These waves

so various, they fall towards you, so many
blues. This beach might soar. The eye counts.

'New Place'

You lie on a bed with three long
thin cats

one white, one ginger, one black
the long brushes

of their tails. While 9000 miles
away

Philip Guston lies with three
tubes of paint

— white, cadmium red, black —
and three

brushes beside him
in his grave.

Mile

At sea, or adrift on a continent
of clouds, wherever this finds you,
wading across the panorama generale,
the boats bearing small orchestras,

mosaic tiles. The scar on your knee,
what oceans assemble there,
what cities of small talk
all lit up? Would you travel this far

for a dentist called Flora Florentino,
to hear Davros and his Sons of Athena
with their Dancing Sisters, to compose
yourself in photographs, among fountains,

palms, to board a bus marked
'Rose Cheek' — a country bordering
you? And the ocean, Gdansk,
did you swim, were you dressed

as a bird for the 'heron dance'?
How your hands have aged, describe
such long hours set on slopes of
night, in foam along a sculpted shore.

Arrival of the departed

Nothing to declare but how small you have become
and thin. Holidays returning on clear bright wheels
as is their fashion. And I am lost to them

as small churches retire to your body, rain removes
the view from the glass — a window
ending there. I need to walk barefoot on

the polished stones which also walk barefoot. I
need a poem called The Light of Dawn at 5pm,
a comb through your hair like a song moving

through its exhausted choir. Passing amidst these
customs, you have brought the warm weather home,
inveterate, you have brought the weather home to stay.

An inexperienced surfer leans into the curl

JESUS EASTER SURF CLASSIC
CHRISTIAN SURFERS NEW ZEALAND, 1992

1

Once again the low tide took
a drastic toll on the waves
and three to four foot peaks became
two foot close outs.

        Without surf
and six hours behind with the
Easter Classic, the organisers
resorted to prayer and Jesus
was called upon to intervene
on behalf of His contest.

2

Was anyone surprised, on the third day
the surf rose,
        the long green wall of
Shipwreck, Larry Fisher milking it,
Shane Grimes at home on the lefts,
Stu Tweedy tearing the top
to pieces,
    getting wild with a
final section, and handling it.

3

The endless face:
Warwick Bliss

zoning in on a
feathering section

carving the high and
fine line.

4

Thanks to everyone involved
for a great weekend,

pure afternoon glass,

and thanks to the Lord
for Easter, and the waves.

5

The Third Day, finding form
on an excellent wave,
               an Unknown
competitor leaning into the curl,
slamming the shorebreak, cutting

the lip. A Red Hot Unknown
firing through a massive floater
at Ninety Mile Beach.

6

So who ripped?

Biography

Every short life's
lasting,
      there are
a number of approaches
to it —
      clouds know most of them.
You clear spaces between the melons
and novels
           to describe them,
then retire to a rock pool

you stare through, a telescope
      or biography
you once read
and wondered who died there,

how their small statues
followed them,
        lovers, children
intent upon their well-being,

how they suffered
tributes, wreaths,
      were gathered
elsewhere, were made
of flesh
      but wandered hence.

Photograph of Maurice Duggan

There being no other way, the road kicks
around to the left, a fine spray

of heather. The lop-sided novelist traces
a line along the ridge, the sun making his face

glisten, eyes tighten, the blonde difficult child
balanced on his head. How did you find

this — the photograph I found on a shelf
among sea-eggs, a pair of scissors washed up

after fifty years, the afternoon its own
composition, brittle, faded? You'd like to see

what the fridge looked like after fifty years under
or left out in the air, how any of us would

look. Skin burnt, layered in salt,
happy? The one-legged man carrying the doctor's

daughter along the Coromandel Ranges, alluvial,
their path or trajectory a seam of quartz,

gold. Part of your education, like falling
down a clay bank. A southerly ruffling the green,

where you stayed once, the pebble beach
clacking. The beautiful cold.

I have found a book to read, *somebody's orchard*,
by somebody my father knew at Sacred Heart College,

but got no further than the drive back to Papakura, rushing
to see Rosemary's eleven puppies before they died.

Leaving those broad shoulders, surprisingly small
hands, ironing the sails. The flapping of sheets

reminding him of his cousin, a nun, shaking
the napkins three times in honour of the Trinity,

while solemnly bowing and intoning: 'I go to bed
as to my grave.' As I recall, theirs being

no other way — you're either burnt or bleached,
how 'we' go to the grave — the child gets down

from the novelist's head, the novelist climbs down
from the Coromandel Ranges, his wooden leg,

the ranges slip down their clay bank, there being
no other way. And this is where I find, Jenny,

between the lop-sided novelist and your
grandmother, we are related.

for Jenny Bornholdt, and in
memory of Maurice Duggan
(1922-74), author of O'Leary's
Orchard & Other Stories

Europe before the war

Lives golden with
dogs

luncheon without shirts
an opening

on a peaceful, feathered
vista

procession with flags, Lee's
'exploding hand'

Alberto's ironwork. A mouse
crosses a continent

a bather climbs into a dark
costume

but who will save
the yachts?

Melancholy sound

1 A native wounded while asleep

Awoke with a length of tree
in his body, his wife and children
a safe distance from the fire.

A spear in his side.
Watched the blood slip through
his skin, go its separate way.

The river slept with his wife,
her prepared spices, decorated
feet. Spear plucked

from his side, he crouched
accusing the stars and boulders.
His beloved turned

in her sleep, her bones shone
under the ghost-footed moon.
Weary now, his blood joins him

to the earth. Tomorrow his skeleton
will be painted on a tree, his shield
buried, a spear thrown hard

into the river.

Botany Bay, 1982

2 'Sleep Light My Fair'

A red mitten half way
up a frozen waterfall

before the snowlit parties
their shoulders and heads

in shadow, skiers crossing
the golfcourse, a snow

boulder containing a
Morris Minor rolling down

the bagpipe-blasted steppes.
As the illuminated feet climb

the frozen waterfall track,
a child is lost in snow,

a child walks down the main
street of a town that never was.

National Park, 1992

Reliquary

Now Eugene is flying home
　　for good, who could tell the hour
by aeroplanes crossing Saint
　　Patrick's, a line of pills

along the dresser; who picked up
　　the ghost of an early
spring morning and shook it
　　this world a small weight

off his back. A windy day, I pinned
　　my drawings to the floor, the eye
adrift with its horizons, tiny
　　splinters of them — you might have

taught me that, Eugene, this life's
　　little work, 'carry home
what you can', to die among
　　indefinable rivers, trees

this far. I was seventeen
　　feet tall at Piha Beach
surf lifted me that high
　　I could see *life* and you just

beyond it, the four loud companions
　　(you would call them 'saints')
beside your hospital bed, those four
　　silent men. The road, Eugene,

is made of stone. I still
　　cannot play the guitar. This
light you will bathe in
　　coming close
　　　　　　to that.

In memory, Eugene O'Sullivan, d. 1988, Ireland

3 Claudio Monteverdi

It is better and more seemly not to beat time with the head, the body nor with the feet. One should have an air of ease at one's Harpsichord, not gazing too fixedly at one object, nor yet looking too vague; in short, look at the assembled company, if there be one, as if not occupied with anything else . . . With regard to making grimaces, it is possible to break oneself of this habit by placing a mirror on the reading desk of the Spinet or Harpsichord . . .

François Couperin, L'Art de Torcher Le Clavecin, *1717*

A man's a genius just for looking like himself.
Thelonious Monk

To love music more than anything . . .
Paul Klee

The conception of C.M.

Given music to describe
what he is describing:
his parents pulled back the folds
    this bed, this harbour.
Childless eleven years
she said
    if we have the warmth
the trade winds
    the materials. If
we could excavate our eleven years
together
            bring forth a child.

Given music to
describe himself
Claudio Monteverdi
    rows drunkenly out
past the breakwater

listens to the small oars
        shout.

*

News of C.M.'s conception reaches home

Shadows nudge her
homewards
    along the street
above the harbour

to tell him she is round
with child (as a choir sings
    a round), that nine months
will yield a composer

that, together
their bodies have
    composed him.

*

C

As a child, was named Claudio
was given the initial C
    after the Middle C
    on the piano. (His mother
said classical music *was a sea*
he could sail off in.)

Before music — and as well as
music — there were the handpainted soldiers
    Monteverdi would organise
into inch-high ranks, designate corporals
ensure adequate provisioning —
    he even wrote a manual on
        the raising of
        troop morale.

Then came music
the orderly formations
    of his compositions
a gift (for the gifted)
from above — as a woman's voice
would descend from the flat above
singing: *Are you the Mr Riley*
        Some speak of so highly . . . ?

And even later, upon hard times
he would join
    the long orderly line
outside a soup kitchen
    aware how the nuns
handing out bowls never distinguished
between a composer, say
    and a waif.

*

The first violinist

Two lovers lay under a bewitched tree and a child was conceived there. When the boy had grown to manhood, one side of his neck began to swell and the shape of a tree soon became evident growing outwards from just below the man's left ear. No one knew how to remedy this unorthodox ailment until, finally, an Orthodox priest suggested all that could be done was to carve the tree into an instrument of music. And that was how a violin came to be balanced peculiarly on the shoulder of the first violinist, where it soon became familiar. And violins have remained similarly, and peculiarly, placed on the shoulders of violinists ever since.

*

As a young man threatened
with the monastery, he maintained

all roads lead to Rome

and, by inference
the other way

*

Monteverdi sent a postcard to his only son, born out of wedlock in a distant country. The postcard had a lighthouse on it and, from that day, the boy always thought of his father as living in a lighthouse.

*

Work delayed by an illness
of the heart
    he prayed for an early recovery
at St Mary of
    (amongst others) the Angels

lit a candle there
for his son
    for his ailing memory
and the ailments of such

a prayer of intercession to the
Blessed Syncletica of Holy Memory
that he might know
    (all there is to know)
'the nature of form
    and how form arises
and how
it perishes'.

*

M:

'I asked the bus-driver
how far I could go
with forty cents in my pocket
and all the madrigals in my heart
the hymns in my soul
all the overtures, choruses
    the endless finales.

He replied forty cents
    and you get as far
as Newmarket.'

*

'A perfect singer
with a heavenly voice'

    the one requirement
the ecology of the world

might yield, reluctantly
    or pour forth

an instrument
love's voice.

*

'Such a mild manner',
his landlady described him
   'such common-
place, a treasure.'
He talked of the need
to know, to sing, Latin
   (a quarter of Paris)
to sway from towers
to one day, perhaps
   meet a woman
to reach for her trembling.
The roof of his atelier
polished by the sun
   as he would say, many skies
gathered there.

*

Claudio & Claudia

The ocean deepest
where their feet would flicker
   blue sky entangled
in their hair. Holding

his hand, she said:
But a truth once seen
   when seen again
will no longer be recognised.
Her parents christened her
   Claudia — a name ending in A
as a Schubert sonata
also ends with the
                  chord of A
                  (Claudia).

He replied his parents, favouring
a girl, planned on calling their
    only child Claudia. Which
led to Claudio, a last-minute revision.

He asked her who wrote:
    To love music
        more than anything
    that is unhappiness.
But she cannot remember the German
painter-violinist's name.
And this is how he remains
unfamiliar to her:

Soon they are gone to a place
where the ocean has nothing
    more to say
but must
go on talking.

*

There were tunes
        madrigals
he tried to forget
'the exotic and irrational
    entertainments'.
There were people he should never
        have mentioned
as a body asleep in bed
    never mentions
        the body beside it.

As children on a beach gather
shells, so Monteverdi, then aged seven
    would gather notes
the layers of sand his stave
each note
    a shell held to the ear.

There were people he continued
to mention
            benefactors, well-wishers
as a body asleep
   in bed always mentions
      the body
            beside it.

*

As Monteverdi left each morning for his atelier, his wife would
wrap a scarf around his neck. Three times around meant she
loved him, she would say, twice meant she had tired of him but
he could stay, and once meant she no longer loved him. But, as
he walked off along the kerb, of course she always loved him.

*

A commission to write the Vespers of the B.V.M.

To make an art of
'pecuniary difficulties
   and spiritual unrest'
the Vespers were to be about
this inability to reason
   this sleeplessness
the fineness of a memory
      recently forgotten.

They were to be about
the one thing — the many
versions of the same —
   as music is all
and must be
         above all
a receptacle of remarkable devotion
   he would compose
in the glass-house or lying on the floor
beneath the mother-of-pearl radiogram.

Music must be an emergency, he noted
it must be
        a flax basket filled with stars.
The pen in his hand writing
one note at a time — the soul being
so simple
it attends to only
           one thing
                at a time.

*

Each day a blonde child would change the flowers by the window at the end of Monteverdi's atelier. The petals were like coloured glass, the light moving through them, fixing them in the memory of the composer.

    Monteverdi always looked up from his desk and smiled at the girl who, unaccountably, ignored him, the frown unflinching on her face.

    Some months went by until, eventually, Monteverdi noticed a smile emerging from the child's face. The smile became more pronounced each day until, some time later, Monteverdi began to leave the room just before the girl's arrival and not resume his place of work until she was gone again.

*

Monteverdi:

'We were
all of us

living in the presence
of grand theories

of such emptiness, vastness
we moved among them

and were moved by them
(as a gull reflected

on a wet roof).
While others changed

their names, their partners
their addresses

we settled here (crossing
among instruments as among

friends). This road
we followed, Claudia, this road

that ran through us
and through our music

this road that was
upon us.'

*

A world so full
of indecision
    observes Monteverdi
how it reaches
so deep into
its reflections
    the folding sea wall
how blue falls
for it
      how blue
      it falls.

*

The singing class

Monteverdi instructed the choir to sing the Vespers *for love* and
for pain, said they were all labourers in the Great House and
this was their great good fortune.

A piece of music, he said, should be composed to fill a specific need for that piece in the world and only if there is a need for that specific piece.

Melancholy. Monteverdi would write the word in the air with his finger. 'In the human brain, smell is the closest sense to memory, closer even than hearing. But music, as well as existing within hearing, is also to do with scent, with flavour. And there is a point where music and memory become one.'

'And composing music is the bringing of a memory to perfection.'

The orderly formations of notes are made disorderly by the composer who relies on his skill and, from elsewhere, a kind of grace 'without which reason forms us crookedly'.

In some languages, not often spoken, Monteverdi said the word for *flowing* of blood was the *walking* of blood around the veins.

He found himself between the possible and impossible worlds — between this world and an imagined other. Although, while composing, Monteverdi maintained music was the only possible world and to exist elsewhere would be impossible.

In some foreign languages he felt at home in, Monteverdi observed that the word for *flowing* of blood was the *playing* of blood in the veins.

His compositions he would describe as being both *architectonic* and a tonic for the architect of these sounds.

*

'As specifics
want to become
   everything'
he gathers
the grandness
   of   of
   each   a
   note   concerto

74

crosses town
on his motorscooter
(a Vespa)
    to compare
his staves with
    the telephone wires
        the power lines
that dissect the city.

*

One night the Blessed Syncletica of Holy Memory appeared
simultaneously in the dreams of three men. It was the evening
Monteverdi embarked upon the composition of his Vespers for
the Blessed Virgin Mary. That afternoon he had watched a man
across the courtyard waiting patiently for a bird to finish
bathing in a public fountain before climbing in himself. The
man, who remained in the fountain all night, was identified the
following day as Pope John XII. And the Church issued a
proclamation that, although a movement was already afoot to
make a saint of her, the Blessed Syncletica had, in fact, never
existed — she had been created out of the 'interplay of some-
one's imagined world and the real world itself'. Although three
men now waking in three separate rooms knew for certain
otherwise.

*

The last time he heard the Vespers
(humming them himself) while walking along

the esplanade, the waves offshore
facing him as he once faced the staves

the music, he fell as a song might fall
between the voices in the children's choir

collapsed on the footpath, raving: I have left
my son on a train I have left my son

on the telephone I have left my son on a ship
passing between islands, beneath the orange leaves

of a tree in autumn. But I have no autumn or winter
to hold him to me, no spring or summer will

warm for me. I have lost my son here, among
the familiar roofs, the familiar boats.

*

Finale

Given the mercy of
the creator
    and that which is
created, his death
was like being caught
    in an updraught.
And it was up to Time
    'the Great Fixer', he said
to fix

nothing. This was the
perfect note
    the bell-like clarity
'as sung from the nose
        and forehead'

and, this way, Monteverdi
was delivered from music
    across the whiteness
blueness
out beyond the overseas terminal

        to music.

*

C.M.'s son:

'My father fell, as out of a dream
from the eye of a lighthouse.
That was how his death
    imagined him.
And I, who never met him
watch the beacon which still
    guides the night-ships
safely past. And this is the form
my years take. But why should
someone I never knew
take hold of my memory?

Some days are bad
    others better
some days seem only
to happen
    somewhere beyond
the rockstrewn hills.'

Island Bay, Wellington

Garden of Love

The schooner Garden of Love, *67 tons, left Wellington for Taranaki on April 21 with crew, three passengers and a valuable cargo. Encountering very bad weather, she was forced to lie at Kapiti Island for several days. During a gale, the schooner parted her cables and, after a vain attempt to keep her off shore with canvas, she was laid on her beam ends by terrific squalls. Her masts went overboard, and she was righted, but one of the passengers, a woman, and a Maori chief named 'Wide-awake', who was clinging to one of the masts, were never seen again. Exposed to a fearful sea, the surviving crew and passengers managed to land, bruised and disabled, from the vessel. The wreckage of the* Garden of Love *was sold to a Levin resident for five pounds eleven shillings.*

Thanks to the editors of the following publications in which many of these poems first appeared: *Scripsi, Meanjin, Landfall, Vital Writing 2 & 3* (ed. Andrew Mason), *NZ Listener, Verse* (UK), *Soho Square IV* (ed. Bill Manhire), *Sport, Literary Half Yearly* (India), *The Caxton Press Anthology of NZ Poetry 1972 – 1986* (ed. Mark Williams), *Printout, Takahe, Island* (Tasmania), and *Poetry New Zealand*.

'Napoli, 32 Vedute' appeared in *Great Lake* (Local Consumption Publications, Sydney, 1991). An earlier version of 'Marsden at Matapouri' appeared in *Dunes and Barns* (Modern House, 1988).

'The Milk Horse' was adapted and produced for broadcast by Radio New Zealand in 1992. An earlier version appeared in the centennial publication of the Home of Compassion Order. It was read at the Wanganui Museum opening of the National Library exhibition, *For Love of God* (curated by Lucy Alcock), in December 1992.

'The New Zealander' and 'Garden of Love' are modified quotations from *Shipwrecks: New Zealand Disasters 1795 – 1936* (Dunedin Book Publishing Association, 1936).

The support of RKS ART, Auckland, and the Bowen Galleries, Wellington, is acknowledged. These poems are a part of the same on-going project as a series of exhibitions of my paintings: *Great Lake* (RKS ART, October 1990), *Days Beside Water* (Bowen, December 1990), *A tarpaulin for Torpedo Sam* (Bowen, December 1991) and *The rockstrewn hills* (RKS ART, July 1992).

Thanks to Andrew Johnston for his technical assistance, to Victor Meertens of Melbourne for pointing me in the direction of Charles Ives's 'The rockstrewn hills', to Anne Kennedy for helping 'Claudio Monteverdi' along its way, to Chris Orsman, Mark Williams, Elizabeth Nannestad and Iain Sharp for support and advice.

These poems span nearly a decade, during which I received a number of project grants from the Literature Committee of the Queen Elizabeth II Arts Council. I also gratefully acknowledge the support of the Frank Sargeson Trust in 1988.

When writing 'Claudio Monteverdi' I knew virtually nothing about the composer's life, apart from the fact that he was a Catholic priest. For the poem I contrived a marriage, between him and an imaginary Claudia, embodying the reconciliation of *male* and *female* elements in the composer's work. Recently I discovered that although Monteverdi was a priest, he had been married and widowed earlier in life. And the name of his wife was, in fact, Claudia.